For John Mullaney
Warmest regards,
Kit Guillon

A BRIDGE TO PEACE

Previous Books by Dr. Cahill

1. *The Untapped Resource: Medicine and Diplomacy*
2. *Health and Development*
3. *Health on the Horn of Africa*
4. *Somalia: A Perspective*
5. *Irish Essays*
6. *The American Irish Revival*
7. *Threads of a Tapestry*
8. *Famine*
9. *The Aids Epidemic*
10. *Tropical Medicine in Temperate Climates*
11. *Tropical Medicine: A Handbook for Practitioners*
12. *Clinical Tropical Medicine – Vol. I*
13. *Clinical Tropical Medicine – Vol. II*
14. *Teaching Tropical Medicine*
15. *Medical Advice for the Traveler*
16. *Health in New York State*
17. *Pets and Your Health*

A BRIDGE TO PEACE

by

Kevin M. Cahill, M.D.

Haymarket Doyma Inc.
New York

Table of Contents

FOR MIGUEL AND NORITA
who kept faith with
the poor and oppressed

INTRODUCTION

A bridge is a blend of poetry and practicality. By appreciating—and harnessing—tensions and forces man can span abysses, link separated lands, and create a thing of beauty. But soaring girders and graceful arches must be firmly anchored in a solid foundation, or even an expected load will collapse, destroying both bridge and travelers.

The imagery of a bridge seems appropriate for those who search for hope in a world where greed and arrogance abound. The prevalence of poverty and political oppression, hunger and disease, prejudice and ignorance can be denied only by the spiritually blind. Somehow the efforts to cross chasms of despair and join the disparate parts of a shattered earth must go beyond the physical. As we struggle against the forces of evil that continue to enslave the vast majority of humanity, we need lofty dreams—bridges of hope —to sustain our lonely steps.

Individual efforts are like a journey into emptiness. Only by forging common bonds can we conquer the gaps that divide us, and only mutual endeavors will build a community where peace, justice, and compassion can thrive. As a physician who has been privileged to share numerous crises with the peoples of the Third World, I have tried, with my writing, to capture the universal experiences of suffering and pain in order to express, for my fellow citizens, the terrible reality of life so often blurred by the obfuscations of politicians.

The articles in this book were written during a five-year period (1982–1987) when circumstances allowed me unusual entree into troubled communities around the world. They were written in the heat of struggle and had to conform to the limited space allowed on newspaper editorial pages. Nevertheless, I hope the reader will find sufficient passion in the sparse style, for outrageous wrongs have been perpetrated in our name. Silence would have been almost as serious a sin as the acts of commission I condemn, and although these essays took unpopular positions it required little courage to identify with those who suffer and die for freedom.

My reflections are based on a foundation of more than a quarter century of clinical and academic work in tropical medicine, and in a philosophy that holds that health, and other humane endeavors, may well be the best—and sometimes the only—tools that can bridge differences and unite warring parties. The geographic distances encompassed within these essays emphasize how similar are the problems around the world and how a non-violent bridge to peace can find application in all societies.

These articles were originally published in *The New York Times, Newsday, America, The Daily News, The*

Journal of Public Health Policy, *Catholic Near East*, and the *Journal of the Royal College of Surgeons in Ireland*.

The reflections of Maestro Leonard Bernstein—whose contributions to music and poetry, civil rights, and religious freedom are legendary—are deeply appreciated.

Louis LeBrocquy, a world-renowned artist and a leader of Amnesty International, has graciously donated the Dove of Peace that appears on the jacket cover.

NICARAGUA

The sovereignty of small nations is usually a myth. Superpowers manipulate client states with such ease that both parties usually recognize the concepts of equality, freedom, and independence as mere rhetoric. Once in a very long while, however, a tiny country will emerge from its own struggle imbued with a revolutionary spirit and the audacity to chart its own path.

Nicaragua paid a terrible price in the 1980s for daring to assert her fundamental national rights. Her land was razed, her economy was destroyed and tens of thousands of her citizens were killed in a sordid mercenary war perpetrated in the name of the American people. I believe the United States also suffered greatly in this conflict, for we tarnished our traditions and divided our people.

I had worked in Nicaragua under different regimes for many years, had shared their euphoria in revolution and knew, more than most, the nobility of their struggle for a dignity that had been raped by generations of oppression. When we tried to crush this impoverished nation, using illegal covert operations coupled with an utter disregard for truth, I felt it would have been un-American not to offer a healing hand and sound a dissenting voice.

1

Respect, Please, for Nicaraguans' Rights

Thomas Jefferson would be at ease in Nicaragua. He understood the need for revolution and an authentic constitution. Unlike those who see all other forms of government as a mortal threat, Jefferson believed, "Each generation has the right to choose for itself the form of government it believes the most promotive of its own happiness."

Today, Nicaragua has a new constitution and an ongoing revolution. The mood, however, is hardly one of national celebration. The major concern is how to understand and deal with a United States administration that is openly committed to overthrowing the Nicaraguan government. I believe such an illicit policy and such immoral behavior underestimates not only

3

the Nicaraguans but the American public.

For two hundred years, the mainstream of America has understood, and always returned to, the fundamentals of Jeffersonian thought. Whenever we had a coherent foreign policy, it was not based merely upon reaction or fear but upon the ideas and ideals that Jefferson expounded. An apparent ignorance of our own history coupled with a cynical and arrogant abuse of false power—false because its foundation is nothing more than shifting expediency—has now tarnished our Jeffersonian image at home as well as abroad.

Fortunately the unreal world of false and bizarre images finally seems to be collapsing as the investigative spotlight exposes our national folly and shame. Today, senior members of both parties in the Congress, and the vast majority of the polled electorate, openly dissent from an official policy based on covert operations, and demand a return to open government.

The public is no longer so insular or innocent to believe that our tradition demands a uniform type of government in other lands, providing Jefferson's "inalienable rights" are respected. The average American can understand a papal hierarchy or regal aristocracy even though he or she may not want to live under such systems. It is the Jeffersonian principles of democracy, and not any particular implementation, that Americans understand best.

There is controversy and confusion in the United

States regarding many aspects of Nicaraguan life, but the average American understands and appreciates the Nicaraguan's struggle against oppression and corruption; he can understand a campaign that has decreased the illiteracy rate from an appalling 50.3 percent to less than 13 percent, and reduced by a third the infant mortality rate from a criminal 113.2 per thousand.

The Nicaraguans share with us basic claims to life, liberty, and the pursuit of happiness. These are not national perquisites that come with power, but are understood by the average American to be universal, fundamental, and non-negotiable claims of humanity.

For the past quarter century, I have been fortunate to serve, usually in the midst of chaos and crisis, the sick, the frightened, the poor and hungry of Africa, Latin America, the Middle East, and Asia. I realized very quickly that neither politicians nor soldiers nor diplomats had a monopoly on wisdom in foreign affairs. My journeys were rarely to resorts, but then again very little that really matters in a world filled with changes and conflict ever happens in resorts.

I have just returned from Nicaragua where I spent my time at a field hospital in a war zone and at a rehabilitation center in Managua examining scores of legless victims of contra mines. I was seared by the pain of groups of mothers whose sons had been mutilated and killed by our own mercenary forces. I saw the effects of an American embargo; surgery must be done and broken limbs set without x-rays because of a belief in Washington that the Sandinista government must be overthrown at any cost.

Our official obsession with this policy has not only caused obvious violations of Congressional intent but has isolated us from a world that believes in the independence and sovereignty of individual nations. We find the United States government, the bastion of the free world, convicted at the International Court of Justice of supporting terrorist activities, mining harbors and delivering lethal weapons, of breaching our obligations under specific treaties and customary standards of international law. We have been ordered by the World Court to "cease and refrain" from contra support, and to pay reparations, and yet we persist in our aggression.

Fortunately, the Administration's approach is at least partly balanced by the thousands of Americans serving Nicaraguans in their struggle for independence. There are more American teachers in Nicaraguan schools than Russians and Cubans combined. American farmers, architects, scientists and artists have become a regular feature of Nicaraguan life.

A physician may have the most privileged role. The intense and intimate relationships of doctor and patient forces both parties to an understanding that is unique; trust and love can evolve in days and be remembered for years. When people and nations can agree on little else, those common bonds become the bridge back to understanding and peace.

My links to Nicaragua go back to the 1972

earthquake. Managua was burning when I arrived only eight hours after the Christmas 1972 earthquake, having responded to a request by the Nicaraguan government to direct the initial disaster relief. I shared a tent with my host, Anastasio Somoza Debayle, but my spiritual guide, then, as now, was the present Foreign Minister, Father Miguel d'Escoto. The scenery was dramatic, the actors incredible and, in retrospect, there was much of the theater of the absurd.

I have made many medical trips to Nicaragua, and by the time the Sandinista Revolution succeeded in 1979 I had already cared for a significant percentage of the present Nicaraguan cabinet members and their families. When Father d'Escoto's health deteriorated last year after a Gandhi-like fast to arouse his country, I traveled to Managua. Barely able to rise from his bed, Miguel said only, "I knew you'd come when the time was right." Maybe, just maybe, I would like to think that the trust that developed and the ideas that were exchanged have helped to sustain a critical perspective during the terrible years of official strain between our nations.

A new constitution has been proclaimed now in Nicaragua in the midst of a war. Friendship and understanding must replace suspicion and hatred as we recall, in the spirit of Jefferson, that the rule of law and the liberties of mankind are what we must all strive for if peace is ever to return to our troubled world. Those basic tenets of civilized society apply to

7

the powerful as well as the weak.

At the beginning of the century, the great Nicaraguan poet, Ruben Dario, wrote:

I seek a form that my style cannot discover,
a bud of thought that wants to be a rose.

Americans should understand and support this dream.

The New York Times, February 14, 1987

The Price
for Differing
With the U.S.
Is Death

The fat lady with severe asthma couldn't breathe and the "Baby Bird," a pediatric machine that was the sole respirator functioning in the largest hospital in Managua, offered only symbolic help. There were six adult respirators in the eight-bed intensive care unit at the Manolo Morales Hospital, but all were broken. The U.S. economic embargo against Nicaragua has interrupted the supply of essential spare parts and prevented the purchase of new machines.

In Nicaragua the price for differing with the United States is death; the contra war is the major direct cause for adult morbidity and mortality, and even the innocent asthmatic dies because of our misguided policies.

There are no sheets or blankets in most medical wards in Managua. There are few bandages and only makeshift splints at the Aldo Chavarria Rehabilitation Hospital. Three weeks ago, I examined dozens of legless victims of contra mines at this sprawling series of tin-roofed sheds that has been converted into one of the busiest hospitals in Nicaragua. The numbers of new amputees outpace the capacity of the three technicians who produce simple wooden limbs. When I made clinical rounds in this hospital six months ago, I examined many of the same patients, and their innocent eyes held an eloquent condemnation I cannot escape.

The diagnostic equipment we take for granted in the United States no longer exist in Managua. Maybe five percent of the microscopes are intact, but it doesn't matter too much since the doctors must diagnose and treat patients with no other laboratory facilities. One cannot measure blood gas levels in any hospital. They have few functioning x-ray machines, but then again almost no x-ray film or developing fluids are available. The more sophisticated scanning equipment has not functioned in years because it is impossible to obtain American spare parts. There is currently an adequate supply of insulin and anti-tuberculosis drugs, thanks to European donors, but vaccines and blood products spoil because the scientific freezers are broken.

Almost all of the modern medical equipment in Nicaragua is of U.S. manufacture. And since compassion and generosity do not appear to be highly rated qualities in our current breed of heroes and leaders, these machines are likely to remain broken and more Nicaraguans will die.

One of the most impressive aspects of the medical picture in Nicaragua is the simple presence of doctors and nurses. Medical personnel are easy migrants, for their skills find a ready market. The fact that they remain at their posts, trying to improvise in a steadily deteriorating setting, speaks volumes for the eight-year-old and ongoing revolution. They stay because they are now part of a national experiment in which the wealth of a previously servile nation has been spread among peasants who were illiterate and had never seen a doctor.

They stay because of deeply spiritual reasons, because they have witnessed a theology that espouses a preferential option for the poor translated into an unparalleled government program of land grants for campesinos who had known only a life of indentured servitude under previous American-supported regimes. They stay, ultimately, because it is their country, with all its warts, and they will not surrender their independence. Our politics of death and destruction are destined to fail because Nicaraguans have tasted freedom and will no longer grovel with a banana republic mentality.

A hospital offers a wonderful cross section of a community, mirroring in its halls and wards not the political rhetoric of statesmen or warriors, but the dreams of a society as well as the realities of a land in conflict and an economy in shambles. The overwhelming impression, at least to this physician who has regularly worked in Nicaragua for fifteen years, is one of a deepening strength and determination. There is an almost palpable pride that permeates the Managua medical scene, and survival, not surrender, is their future.

We, the most powerful nation on earth, a country built by those who fled oppression, should understand Nicaragua's right to be free. Our American heritage has not been built on conquering the weak; armed intervention in other lands is alien to the democratic traditions we cherish. Yet we, the United States of America, have been convicted in the International Court of Justice of supporting terrorism, mining harbors and killing and maiming innocent civilians in Nicaragua. The contra forces are a shameful creation of administration policy.

To invoke the words used recently by a lieutenant colonel with a distorted sense of history, "for the love of God and the love of our country," let us cease killing and begin to foster healing and peace.

Newsday, August 21, 1987

Holidays
in Nicaragua

It was difficult to find reasons for celebration this past Thanksgiving in Nicaragua. Even the Miskito Indians, returning from refugee camps in Honduras, were delayed, and my romantic plans for dinner with them never materialized. I doubt that anything has ever been on time in Puerto Cabezas.

Thanksgiving is a uniquely American holiday and citizens living overseas normally parade their identity and share, in a symbolic meal, their good fortune. In Nicaragua today there are few reasons for joy; to be an American there on Thanksgiving was almost embarrassing. The U.S.-supported contra forces continue to murder, rape, and terrorize, while the national economy has collapsed under our embargo. The signs of death, destruction, and abject poverty are every-where—hardly the setting for a Thanksgiving feast.

Yet traditions are important in our lives, and only a sense of history and a belief in the mercy of God made this Thanksgiving Day tolerable. I left the capital city of Managua—where I had been attempting to resurrect, for the government, a health system crippled by war—and traveled to the Atlantic coast town of Puerto Cabezas.

Prosperity is a relative term, and there are few surprises for a tropical medicine specialist who has worked in numerous refugee camps during the past quarter-century. But the initial—and lasting—impression of Puerto Cabezas is one of long-suffering tinged by perverse incongruities and life-saving humor. Nature and war have been unkind parents.

It is a town of ramshackle wooden houses set on stilts over a malarious marsh. There is no running water, no telephone, no television, only occasional and sparse electrical service and no fire department. Conflagrations fanned by the Atlantic winds seem to be a regular phenomenon that the local population accepts as part of their fate. There is one paved street. At the intersection, near the school, hangs a huge traffic light. It doesn't work, but the town leaders are very proud of it and believe it symbolizes urban progress to the Indian tribes that come in to trade from the Rio Coco and its tributaries.

Clinical rounds in the local hospital offered the best insight into the reality—and courage—of Puerto

Cabezas. A tin-roofed shed, built seventy-five years ago, houses those desperate enough to seek medical care. I had a bizarre conversation with a German-born surgeon who firmly refused "to operate any more without anaesthesia; they move too much, I just can't do it." Since the U.S. economic embargo went into effect five years ago, there are chronic shortages in every sector of society, but nowhere can the impact be felt more clearly than at the hospital.

There is often no anaesthesia; the respirators and x-ray machines cannot function because essential spare parts are victims of our blockade. Shortages of bandages and plaster make homemade casts and traction splints worthy of a Rube Goldberg. The intensive-care unit appeared to be so designated because there were two blood pressure cuffs and a fan; there was no other equipment in the room. Tuberculosis is rampant, but appropriate drugs are in short supply. The antibiotics we take for granted do not exist in the real world of Puerto Cabazas. There mothers and babies die of treatable infections because a U.S. President wants Nicaragua to "cry uncle."

The Reagan Administration apparently believes that our government, sprung from Pilgrims who once shared their bounty with Indians, has somehow inherited the right to dictate how others should live. If the poor and hungry and diseased citizens of Nicaragua do not accept our direction then, according to our current leaders, it is justified in unleashing mercenary forces to murder and destroy in the name of democracy.

15

Returning to Managua, thinking of the next holiday we are already planning in our safe and comfortable society, I could only hope that history will be kind to us. Maybe future scholars will recall that while misguided politicians inflicted terrible pain on innocent women and children, and severely tarnished our own traditions, thousands of American volunteers came to Central America. Farmers and contractors, clergy and medical workers, young enthusiasts and retirees who lost their own children in Vietnam give witness today in Nicaragua to the American heritage we like to recall at Thanksgiving and Christmas.

There is a movement for peace throughout Central America, but it demands that we stop supporting the contra rebels. One can no longer indulge in the obscene—and deadly—games of defining helicopters and military training as humanitarian aid. We must recapture the true spirit of America, one built on tolerance, understanding and a sharing of our wealth with those less fortunate—regardless of their color or religion or traditions.

We must give peace a chance to take seed in the rubble we have created in Nicaragua. There may be, if we allow it to happen, a Second Coming during this Christmas season when, to paraphrase Yeats, peace like a rough beast, its hour come round at last, slouches toward Bethlehem to be born.

America, January 9, 1988

A Bridge
to Peace

The current American policy toward Nicaragua poses a fundamental challenge to those who consider themselves the leaders of our public health. Those who absent themselves from the present national debate, who seek anonymity in silence, who fear to venture forth from their safe harbors and shoals of academia, will have sacrificed a rare opportunity as professionals and as citizens.

Too rarely have health professionals been willing to venture into the rough-and-tumble world of public life where the protective coat of our specialized knowledge has sadly been more of a shield than a sword. Albert Einstein once indicted his professional colleagues thus: "Intellectuals," he said, "are cowards,

even more than most people. They have failed misera-
bly when called on to fight for dangerous convictions.
Anyone who seeks to affect the course of events must
exert direct influence on men and their activities." In
bringing some balance to what I believe is a serious
distortion of America's heritage, a foreign policy that
violates almost every principle we were once taught
to treasure, health workers may be an untapped
resource.

Public health professionals are among the most
educated and, occasionally, the most respected members of a community. Yet, except when an issue
impinges on their particular interest, their impact on
government policy is miniscule. A physician may have
the most privileged role, especially in societies where
there are multiple reasons for suspicion or cynicism or
even hatred. By a mutual sharing, the good physician
becomes part of the body and soul of the person he
serves. If that trust and confidence are not abused, and
if, with warmth and humility and competency, the
doctor proves his worth over time, the bond becomes
as durable as love. When people and nations can agree
on little else, those common bonds may become the
bridge back to understanding and peace. There is
certainly no reason not to utilize this bridge, especially
in light of the dismal record of standard diplomacy.
There are precedents for this approach.

Six of the signers of the Declaration of Independence were physicians, and one of the founders of
modern public health, Hermann Biggs, unabashedly

worked his miracles within a political context. He blatantly utilized the credibility secured by serving as physician to a Tammany Hall leader in order to change not only the administration of health care but of child labor laws and education and sanitation projects. Where there had been a dearth of medical initiative, innovation and even thought, he brought a new vision in which the health worker was pivotal in fashioning a just society. He fought, as a citizen, for the right of the weak and the poor, capturing—for those who had not seen and did not know—the pangs of hunger, the pain of illness, and the burden of ignorance and illiteracy.

Today, as health professionals, we have a unique opportunity. We cannot afford to be so well insulated by distance and by our own good fortune that we no longer feel the chill reality of others' sufferings. We must not allow the facts of hunger and poverty, of disease and oppression to remain merely statistics and forget that it is people, not numbers, who get sick and are starving and brutalized. We must not merely talk about problems and deceive ourselves that words—or even concern—are a substitute for corrective actions and deeds of compassion. Somehow we must translate our impotent sense of outrage into a force that can challenge current political decision-making.

The clamor of those who seek solutions in armed conflict is rarely balanced in public forums by those who believe America can best be served by healing hands that will bind the wounds of mistrust and hatreds that only perpetuate our suffering. Those entrusted with public health are a faint echo of their potential and tradition, a tinkling cymbal in a concert dominated by the banging drums of those who see communists under every bush, and the loud horns of those who somehow believe the United States enjoys a divine right to dominate all aspects of our neighbors' lives.

As our sordid involvement in the Nicaraguan war becomes ever more clear, as the mercenary contra forces continue to mine and kill and rape with American support, we, once the bastion of the free world, find ourselves ever more isolated from civilized opinion and have been found guilty of terrorism by the International Court of Justice.

Americans can ignore Nicaragua today only by abandoning their responsibility as citizens. In the 1930s we could and, to a great extent, did deny an involvement in Nazi Germany, but we bore the eventual burden of millions of Jews who were killed without our objections. In the 1960s it was not the military losses but moral questions that galvanized America's concerns about our Vietnam policy. So in the 1980s does Nicaragua pose a choice.

I have visited that small nation many times in the past decade and a half, and have had the rare opportunity to observe the spirit of her people in major crises. In 1972/3 I directed Nicaragua's health services after the devastating earthquake that destroy-ed the capital city of Managua, killing some twenty thousand people in a night. Subsequent journeys exposed me to the struggles of priests, students, and peasants. They sought the basic freedoms and human dignity we take for granted, and their revolution succeeded in 1979.

Health was a major priority of the new government, and in the first few years over half the national budget went to medical and educational programs. But since 1981 I have seen those dreams distorted by forces beyond their control. The covert contra army, an embarrassing creation of the Reagan Administration, pursues its destructive goals not by military confrontation but by attempts to unravel a fragile society. Health facilities and workers are prime targets.

Over one hundred hospitals and clinics have been selectively razed by the contras; some forty-one civilian doctors and nurses in rural areas have been killed, and thirty-three others have been kidnapped and are presumed dead. In a country of only three million people, the contra war in the last seven years has claimed over forty thousand dead and wounded, and two hundred fifty thousand peasants have been displaced. The American economic embargo has denuded hospitals; there are, for example, few x-ray machines still functioning, and even anesthesia is no longer available in many centers. The most poignant indications of America's impact on Nicaragua today are the legless victims of contra mines.

By March 1986, some 676 young people, the majority being innocent coffee-pickers, were missing one or both lower limbs. I have seen these teenagers waiting in humble hospitals for wooden legs and have been seared by their silent stares.

Are we a nation whose principles are no deeper than "might is right"? Can we, as a people, isolate ourselves from our own government's murderous deeds done in the name of democracy? Can we afford merely to be bemused by double-talk and twisted logic? If the Congress of the United States votes against contra aid, who has empowered the President's staff to then ask, in our name, for tens of millions of dollars from other nations who are simultaneously seeking our favor? And then to make matters more ludicrous, his minions manage to lose the money. Do we really want a foreign policy for Nicaragua based on maintaining illicit pressure until, in President Reagan's pithy phrase, they "cry uncle"?

When did we inherit the right to dictate to other nations what forms of government they may have, when and how their elections should be held, and who should be permitted to lead them? Are our neighboring nations respected as sovereign and independent or do we view them merely as our backyard to be "managed" solely to our advantage? Should we, even if it seems to satisfy immediate needs, use our vast resources to crush the aspirations of those oppressed in other lands? Have we learned nothing from Vietnam? Do we still believe it is right—or even possible—to impose our perception of morality on others, particularly if they have already experienced generations of colonialist domination? Will new nationalists, anywhere, ever again grovel as citizens of "banana republics"? And why should they?

These—and many other—questions we all ask in the privacy of our hearts and our homes. But education and social position offer a different option for those priviliged to direct the public health of a nation. This is not a time for silence or self-delusion. It is a time when the responsibility of our profession demands that we try to restore the heritage of honesty and compassion that once characterized America.

Journal of Public Health Policy, Autumn, 1987

Fasting
and Medicine
in Nicaragua

Medicine is a rare profession, possibly the only one that can permit immediate and total access where suspicion and even hostility might be expected. Deep national differences do not divide the physician and the patient, and the bridge to understanding that seems so elusive for politicians and diplomats caught in an endless power game may be found in the common concerns of shared pain, suffering, and healing.

This conviction that medicine offers a rare opportunity for international diplomacy was set forth in *The Untapped Resource* (1971) issued by the Maryknoll publishing house, Orbis Books. I was the author, and the Rev. Miguel d'Escoto, M.M., was the publisher.

Now he is Foreign Minister of Nicaragua, and I, an American physician, was trying to manage the medical complications of his almost month-long total fast.

Father d'Escoto had been drinking only water in a spiritual exercise he hoped would call attention to the effects of American foreign policy on his nation. The thesis we had developed so passionately fourteen years earlier now offered a personal opportunity for implementation.

The level of mutual misunderstanding and inflammatory rhetoric seen in recent U.S.-Nicaraguan communications faded as I measured falling blood pressure and decreasing urinary output. Mixed in with discussions on the effects of starvation were dialogues on the meanings of freedom, democracy, and independence.

The stethoscope was a symbol of decency and offered a key to an embattled land where a young government was attempting to deal in its own independent fashion with inherited problems of poverty, ignorance, and disease unrivaled in Central America.

The trust and confidence that greeted me in Nicaragua might be attributed to my medical services that date back to the Managua earthquake of 1972. But I would suspect that it reflected a more universal desire for peace with dignity, a preference for dialogue rather than destruction, and a belief that tolerance, even generosity, should be expected from a great nation dealing with a determined and proud but poor and admittedly inexperienced government.

Between visits to Father d'Escoto I had hours of conversation with President Daniel Ortega and met spiritual leaders—bishops, priests, and nuns—from all over Latin America who were fasting in union with Father d'Escoto.

Something profound was happening in that simple church shed with its unpainted corrugated roof and leaking walls. Embodied in the skeletal frame of a fasting priest were the frustrations and bitterness of long-oppressed campesinos and those who fought for their basic human rights. Mixed with the stagnant smell of a tropical sick room was the warm perfume of love. A confidence that the aspirations of Latin America were about to be realized permeated the congregation.

It may be difficult to measure the force that emanates from such a gathering, but I suspect the changing political winds sweeping Peru and Uruguay, Brazil and Argentina have been further fanned by the fast of Miguel d'Escoto, and they will not fade. The spiritual tool so effectively used by Gandhi was again unifying downtrodden peoples across parochial borders.

These experiences in Nicaragua confirm my belief that medicine—and other humane endeavors—offer an untapped resource in international diplomacy. Many physicians may feel uncomfortable stepping beyond the safe and standard parameters of clinical care. I certainly do not suggest that the mere acquisition of a health degree equips one for the delicate discipline of diplomacy, especially in the volatile world of the tropics. Yet the history and philosophy of medicine do support those who, with sensitivity and knowledge and humility, realize there are no rigid bounds to the definition of our profession.

The trust and confidence accorded the physician may serve as one of the new bridges so desperately needed in our mutual efforts toward greater security and peace. In understanding and serving the dreams of the starving, we may find solutions—or at least approaches—where traditional methods have failed.

America, September 7, 1985

The University
and Revolution

Universities reflect the societies they serve. At all times universities try to teach the young to learn and to accept the burden of leadership; they prepare a new generation to take the torch of responsibility and educate those who must expand society's vision while preserving its traditions. In times of political stability, the university, the repository of historical and cultural wisdom, becomes the focus for the refinement of all that makes a civilization. During times of national groping, as in the United States during the Vietnam War, the university can become the center for dissent, coalescing the philosophic concerns of elders with the rebellious resistance of youth. During times of revolution, a university, particularly a Catholic and Jesuit university, must fill all these roles and do even more—it must somehow capture the dreams of the liberated, translate the soul of the struggle, and define for a skeptical world the goals of rebellion.

There is nothing terribly new in this mandate. Cardinal John Henry Newman, in his *Idea of a University*, summarized these aims a century ago: "A university training is the great ordinary means to a great but ordinary end; it aims at raising the intellectual tone of society, at cultivating the public mind, at purifying the national taste, at supplying true principles to popular enthusiasm and fixed aims to popular aspiration, at giving enlargement and sobriety to the ideas of the age, at facilitating the exercise of political power...."

Cardinal Newman's noble goals were not conceived in worldly security. They were delivered in 19th-century Dublin where bigotry, discrimination, and economic exploitation denied Irish Catholics access to academia. They reflected the revolutionary dreams of the poor; they were a cry for decency and dignity, a demand for quality and equality. If they were born in isolation and rejection, they have, nonetheless, grown into the universal ideals of higher education.

It is important to recall the humble origins of Cardinal Newman's *Idea*, for it may serve a Latin America in need of courage. As Julio Cortázar (1914–84), an Argentinian poet and novelist, has so beautifully noted, "The reality of Latin America... is almost

30

always agitated and tormented. There are situations of oppression and shame, of injustice and cruelty, of the submission of entire peoples to relentless forces bent upon maintaining them in a state of illiteracy.... It is on this field, stained with blood, torture, imprisonment, and degrading demagoguery, that literature—and universities—wage battles, as on others they are waged by visionary politicians and activists who often give their lives for a cause that may seem utopian to many but is not."

It is within the great tradition of Newman and the passionate counsel of Julio Cortázar that the University of Central America (UCA) has assumed such a prominent place in the intellectual life of Nicaragua today. This independent seat of learning has opted for social involvement as its method of perfecting the revolution and has made its resources available for the development of the nation; it fashions the response of an educated urban elite to the problems of slum dwellers and campesinos.

There can be no barriers at the campus gates for a university in a revolution. If the special needs of the poor and social justice for all are the goals of a revolution, then a university must mirror these aspirations or wither away in irrelevancy. Entrusted with the minds and imaginations of the young, a university cannot survive as an island; training students in social-action projects is as legitimate a part of a first-rate education as is teaching them the classics.

Robert Kennedy once noted that the future is not

a gift, but an achievement that has to be earned, that the future does not belong to those who are content with today, but neither does it belong to those who are content to forget the past. Linking the academic curriculum and professional staff of a university with the needs of a community in revolution promotes current progress while preserving traditional values.

Ideally the university should be able to reach these dual goals unfettered. Some six hundred years ago, St. Thomas Aquinas and the teachers' guild in Paris (all of whose members were clerics) developed the concept of the university, or *studium*, as a third force that has a necessary independence from the civil authority, or *regnum*, and the ecclesiastical authority or *sacerdotium*. In a revolution the university cannot afford to be divorced from the struggle, but it also cannot allow itself to become the handmaiden of a political party or particular ideology. The university must be free in its search for truth and in its ability to analyze events constructively and to criticize theories effectively.

Its very nature rebels against the imposition of either secular or religious orthodoxy. In preserving its essential independence the university protects the fundamental goals of a revolution, those fragile dreams of freedom that must be nourished by debate or die. With concentrated wisdom and understanding it can emerge as the true alma mater, assisting in the formation of a conscience for the nation, guiding the leaders of the present and molding the minds of future generations.

This is not an easy task. The rector of UCA, César Jérez, S.J., in his acclaimed Notre Dame address last year, expressed the challenge of UCA in trying to reach those who have "become numb through suffering, silent through fear, skeptical through disillusion, or so absorbed by the daily task of survival as to be incapable of other preoccupations." Yet if freedom and liberty are to be realized, an educated citizenry is more essential to an ongoing revolution than weapons. Both partners in a marriage make commitments, and while the university can assist government with social projects, the state must manifest its belief in education by example and support.

One of the most remarkable demonstrations of the critical importance of a university to a revolution is the current effort of President Daniel Ortega to continue his law studies. Having abandoned his formal education in 1965 to participate in an armed struggle for independence, he has now returned to complete the academic demands of the legal profession and, in doing so, he offers a unique lesson to his country. Neither the military nor the presidency confer degrees; a university establishes standards in education, and even the most powerful must seek its recognition. That lesson of mutual respect and co-operation is being watched around the world.

What the superior general of the Society of Jesus, Peter-Hans Kolvenbach, S.J., said in a sermon he gave in Caracas, Venezuela, on October 12, 1984, can surely be applied to the work of UCA: "It is Latin America that has opened the eyes of all Jesuits to the preferential love for the poor and to the fact that the true, integral liberation of men and women must take priority as the focus of the mission of the Society of Jesus today." As so often happens in history, Jesuit educators are once again on that borderline where the church meets the world. The business of a university is knowledge. Sharing that knowledge with a nation striving toward the basic rights of literacy and health will guarantee UCA a place of pride when the history of the revolution can ultimately be written. May that day of peace come soon.

America, August 22, 1987

Laudatio on Conferring an Honoris Causa *Doctorate on Kevin M. Cahill, M.D., at the Universidad Centroamericana*

Cesar Jerez, S.J.

The Universidad Centroamericana (UCA) has granted two *honoris causa* doctorates in the past eight years: one to President Carter and the other to you, Dr. Cahill. Some colleagues of the academic world have said, with a certain irony, that this university is specializing in granting honorary degrees to deserving U.S. citizens. "Specializing" is perhaps overstating the case for two degrees, albeit the only such ones granted, in a period of eight years.

Speaking theoretically, it is not an easy decision for a Nicaraguan university to confer an honorary degree on a citizen of the United States, bearing in mind the painful circumstances of our country. At the same time, speaking dialectically, this act is an unmistakable demonstration of the clear distinction that the Nicaraguan people have made during the last eight years: The administration of the United States is not the people of the United States. You have expressed this distinction with clarity.

It is an honor for the Universidad Centroamericana to confer this degree on you for many reasons, which I wish to sum up in three points:

1. There is a clear parallel between what you are and what this university aspires to be. I say aspires because we cannot claim that our aspirations have been realized: The Universidad Centroamericana supports profound social change. This support can be expressed by the university in the following ways: (a) teaching; (b) research; (c) social involvement; (d) being a critical and creative consciousness in the transformation process; and (e) safeguarding the cultural values of Nicaraguan society. By virtue of being a university of Christian inspiration, governed by the Society of Jesus, it endeavors to complete these tasks demanded by the national reality and by the values of the Gospel in the special way the Latin American Church has called "the preferential option for the poor."

As a former student of the Jesuits and as a close friend, you know us, Dr. Cahill. You know that St. Ignatius Loyola, the founder of our Order, bid the Jesuits to be men of thought and great aspirations, to take up work in the frontier. During the last four centuries and more, this boldness has been very costly for us: expulsions, imprisonments, martyrdoms, calumnies, and even revelations of our own deficiencies to the very point of the temporary suppression of the Society of Jesus. I said that a fundamental reason for conferring this honorary degree is the parallel that I see between what you, Dr. Cahill, are and what the UCA aspires to be. Without intending to wound your modesty, I must point out that you are a renowned scientist. You have written some twenty books and about two hundred articles; all of this is a result of your teaching, your research, your love of culture.

2. There is a special role played in your scientific genius by your Christian faith, your love for the poor. This love has transformed itself into an effective dedication to the cause of the dispossessed. We can call this your profound Christian humanism.

Nicaragua is at war. The blood of its youth, the blood of its poor is being shed daily. Only a very few days ago, on July 3rd, our Franciscan brother, Friar Tomás Zavaleta, was killed by a mine, and Franciscan Father Ignacio Urbina and two companions were wounded. We would be a deficient church if we did not mingle the blood of priests, religious, catechists, delegates of the Word, and simple believers with the blood of the poor. These sad events lend themselves to diverse interpretations according to ideological orientations: Some say that this is a conflict among Nicaraguans and that the solution is the reconciliation of the native-born brothers and sisters; others say that

Nicaragua is suffering the consequences of the East/ West confrontation. In my opinion, which coincides with yours, the crucial point is the decision of the present administration of the United States to put an end to this Revolution that also seriously aspires— although there are some deficiences—to take the preferential option for the poor to its ultimate conse- quences. In your profound Christian humanism you have understood the crux of the matter very well. It seems to me that the moment is coming, after the errors and atrocities committed by the White House, of a greater commitment by the civilian population of the United States: members of the churches, the pacifist movements, the unions, the universities.

You are a special representative of those I call the civilian population of the United States. Your Irish ancestry, of which I am well aware, has allowed you to understand the rights of the small countries of this world. As you have written:

> The Irish tragedy is not just an internal affair
> of the British government but a moral affront
> to the entire world community.

Your profound Christian humanism has brought you to a similar view about the position of the White House with respect to the Sandinista Revolution.

You have wanted that medicine be for you a diplomatic tool at the service of peace. We know that you use medical science when attending heads of state, North American politicians, high-ranking church functionaries, including Pope John Paul II, as well as missionaries serving the poor in the Third World. We also know that at the same time you try to encourage these notables to be instruments of peace. You know Nicaragua and its deep commitment to peace very well. Perhaps this is the reason for the love and dedication that you have shown to Nicaragua's cause, which is the cause of the poor of this earth.

For your many scientific achievements and for your profound Christian humanism, the Universidad Centroamericana takes special pleasure in conferring upon you the degree of Doctorate in Humanities. We do not house a faculty of medicine, but in my opinion you have placed medical science at the service of humanism.

3. Dr. Cahill, I would like to end by saying that in your case there is a familiar cause for joy in conferring this honorary degree. While Jesuit education has many defects and has been harshly criticized, one must point out that, omitting mentioning the names of many who are present here, there have passed through the halls of Jesuit institutions such personages as Fidel Castro, Jaruzelski, Buñuel, Hitchcok, Descartes, Corneille, Voltaire, Charles de Foucauld ... and you as well, Dr. Cahill.

Universidad Centroamericana, Managua, Nicaragua, July 16, 1987

THE MIDDLE EAST

In the past decade Lebanon and Libya have become synonyms for anarchy. Conditions in these countries were not always chaotic. In the early sixties, when I worked for several years as a physician in the Arab world, Beirut was known as the "Paris of the East" while the towns and oases of the Western Desert reflected an ancient and stable culture.

What we hold as "truth" in the modern world is often a bias offered by the media which, in turn, is based on an uncritical acceptance of self-serving political press releases. Was Lebanese society fatally flawed by centuries-old internecine struggles? Were all Palestinians terrorists? Were Israeli bombing actions immune from questioning? Should patent lies be accepted as a justification for attacking Libya merely because one did not like her leader? These questions— and other equally unpopular ones—demanded to be asked, particularly if one could bring an eyewitness perspective to the discussion.

41

Beirut's
Smell of Death

Armenian scholars no longer search for God in the Near East School of Theology in West Beirut. The cool archives room in the cellar is now a blood bank, and the conference hall where ecclesiastical nuances were once the topic of discussion now contains two operating tables for assembly-line amputations and a bin for severed limbs.

This month the Palestinian Red Crescent Society incorporated the School of Theology into one of the most remarkable health-care delivery services in the world, one that maintains twenty-five dispensaries and a two thousand-bed hospital system serving a half million people still surviving the air and ground attacks that threaten the existence of west Beirut. The world-famous American University of Beirut Hospital is the backup center for the field hospital at the theology school, and I had the privilege of examining patients and consulting with doctors in both places last week. Medicine is that rare discipline that permits almost instant acceptability by all sides in a conflict. It offers a unique perspective on war, as close as one gets to the viewpoint of the victim.

I undertook a tour of the war-ravaged areas of Lebanon at the request of Terence J. Cardinal Cooke, who is president of the Catholic Near East Welfare Association. Accompanied by Msgr. Edward Foster of the Pontifical Mission, I worked in that scarred and tortured land once fabled for its beauty. Square blocks of the ancient biblical cities of Tyre and Sidon have been bombed away. We could not find a single intact structure—nor a single person—in the formerly Christian town of Damur, and Israeli bulldozers were wiping away evidence that Palestinian camps, once home for tens of thousands of families, even existed.

Statistics are a game that politicians play in war. People far from the scene are having a great debate in the American press about the accuracy of death figures in Lebanon. But there is nothing subtle about the current carnage in Beirut if one can recognize blood or smell a festering wound or feel the feverish head of a dying child. There is no mystery about the scope of this tragedy if one walks the wards of the university hospital of the School of Theology and sees the limbless bodies, the fractured faces, the blind, the burned. These are real people, men and women and children, hundreds of them, and no amount of sophistry can dehumanize the horrors of this war into a sterile column of figures. They were not numbers I examined; they were the innocent civilian debris of a war not of their making, but caused by policies that have left them a stateless people. Now they have their dead and their maimed to nourish their hatred and determination.

We saw young refugees in Tripoli in the far north of Lebanon who had traveled hundreds of miles over mountains only to find that their parents were lost somewhere on the trek. The frightened, almost hopeless stare of a hungry orphan can tell a great deal about the wisdom of war. I met an Austrian woman whose husband and two children were gone when she returned home from her job as a nurse in west Beirut. They lived in a camp that had been destroyed by incendiary and cluster bombs. "I could find no one," she said, "only bits and pieces of arms and legs. We just pushed the whole camp into a hole and covered it with plastic and earth." Wherever we traveled, official statistics released by the occupying forces referred only to Lebanese casualties, so one often heard ludicrously low estimates. It was as if the Palestinians —those hundreds of thousands of women and children who had nothing to do with Palestine Liberation Organization fighters—simply did not exist.

Aid is received by the governing authorities only for displaced Lebanese who, to be sure, deserve international help, for they have suffered inordinately since the civil war broke out in 1975. The occupying forces refuse, however, to accept any direct assistance for Palestinians, stopping even food and medicines from being taken to the ravaged, rat-infested ghettos of west Beirut.

Unless the indiscriminate bombing and shelling cease for good, the load of shattered limbs discarded from the Near East School of Theology will grow. While the wise men struggle slowly with the semantics of peace, panic-stricken victims scream psychotically in halls where scholars once pondered the words of God. Hatred abounds and the legacy of bitterness that will be reflected a generation hence in cripples on the streets of Beirut will pose a greater threat to the security of the area than militaristic minds seem capable of considering now.

The painful process toward reconciliation and eventual peace may be best symbolized today in the joint efforts at healing by Armenians, Palestinians, Christian and Moslem Lebanese, Norwegian volunteers, and this American who shall long remember the privilege of making clinical rounds in the Near East School of Theology. Examining patients while shells exploded and fires raged nearby, and with the sick smell of death and disease overwhelming my senses, I wondered what ends could ever justify these means.

The New York Times, July 24, 1982

A Doctor's Reflections
on the Libyan Situation

American planes were bombing Libya last week as I
was completing a medical mission to Yemen. For
a quarter of a century I have had the privilege of
working part of each year in the "developing" lands of
Africa, Latin America, and the Mideast, serving as a
physician during epidemics and in refugee camps,
amid the chaos of natural disasters ranging from
floods and droughts to earthquakes and famines. My
view of these lands, with the smells, sounds and
feelings of naked, exposed human beings, must be the
opposite of the bombardier seeing that reality,
through missile sights, as faceless targets and goals.

Having seen twenty-five years ago how the
greatness and beauty of America were distorted

abroad when presented solely through military and commercial ventures, I proposed we take advantage of the understanding and goodwill that flow from shared humane endeavors. I discovered, in the Mid-east of the early 1960s, that even when there were few areas for agreement, it was still possible to focus on common convictions—that mothers and babies, for example, should be nourished and housed.

On those unfilled and basic needs, bridges can be built as a mutually beneficial alternative to endless recriminations and threats. These ideas took root and flourished for a period among internationalists in the United States, but seem now to be fading fast in the afterglow of neoisolationism that sees America's destiny more in terms of East-West conflict than North-South accommodation.

Once again, we are beginning to convince ourselves that we have the right to dictate to other nations rather than win their support by sharing, or at least understanding, their problems. Once again, we apparently see no wrong in arrogating for ourselves the self-anointed roles of international judge and enforcer. History does not indicate that we will be treated kindly. The worldwide acclaim Israelis won when they captured Adolf Eichmann, convicted him in a court of law and executed him for crimes against humanity can be contrasted with the loss of esteem and the international condemnation that followed the indiscriminate bombing of Beirut, and the Shabra and Shatila refugee-camp slaughters. No matter how frustrated a major nation becomes, it cannot take revenge on innocent people without paying a terrible price. That is the failed policy of the jungle, and it destroys the integrity and legitimacy of a nation at home and abroad. We condemn terrorism against our civilians, but those we kill in revenge are just as dead as the American victims and, it turns out, usually just as innocent.

In reflecting on America's response, I do not justify Libyan—or any other—violations of our inherent right to live in safety and without fear. But we will not secure that by abandoning the rich traditions and principles that are the essence of America. We cannot let truth become the victim of expediency without even a comment. It was appalling to arrive home and realize how minimal were the editorial questions raised about the Libyan exercise, for it was almost as if it would be anti-American to voice concern in the middle of a patriotic orgy. When the President declared that he had never intended to kill Muammar el-Qaddafi—or even overthrow him—it was surprising that not a single newspaper or TV commentator in my orbit asked why bombs fell on his home repeatedly, killing his daughter and wounding his sons. Truth is an essential quality for credibility with our allies, and discussion and dissent are necessary in a free society.

To maintain the civilization we enjoy, we cannot resolve differences by disregarding international law. We are obsessed with our own anger but seem incapable of appreciating the validity of others' hostility. We do no service to the search for peace by labeling our opponents "mad" or "terrorists." Terrorism will continue to be a method in the Mideast conflict as long as the Palestinian problem remains an open wound. Generations have survived in refugee camps in that area because of political decisions beyond Palestinian control, and terrorism will flow from that bitter well, with or without Libyan Colonel Qaddafi. Guerrilla tactics have always been the recourse of the underdog when competing with superior opponents, and we shall not change that approach by retaliation alone. The simplistic solutions of a Rambo—even if applauded for the moment by an emotional public—will ultimately fail. The tide of history is against those who believe that military might can prevail. Only the hand of healing will bind the wounds of mistrust and division that prolong our suffering.

America, May 3, 1986

NORTHERN
IRELAND

Hatred and bigotry—and their progeny, oppression and terrorism—are not restricted to the Third World. One of the longest lasting guerrilla conflicts continues to destroy Belfast and Derry. Ireland, the land of my ancestors, holds a special claim on my spirit. Good fortune has allowed me to be deeply involved in Irish affairs on both sides of the Atlantic.

For the past two decades I have traveled, four times a year, to Ireland, North and South, as Professor of International Health in Dublin; simultaneously I have served as President-General of the American-Irish Historical Society in New York. The dual positions offered an opportunity—as well as a responsibility—to help define America's role in the current Irish conflict. Most of my views on this topic have already been published in an earlier volume, *Irish Essays*, but periodic observations, such as those presented here, reflect my continued sense of both failure and optimism.

Red Stains on
the Emerald Isle:
Can Only Blood
Wash Them Out?

There is a blood-red strand—dark and evil—that runs through the tapestry of Irish history. Amid the soft hues of saints and scholars, side by side with the rich colors of bards and poets, are streaks of violence, torn threads representing sudden death and wanton destruction.

That perverse part of the Irish scene is perpetuated today not merely by fanatics intent on imposing their own peculiar view of justice through the barrel of a gun or the blast of a hidden bomb, or even by those simplistic partisans who, far from danger, glorify killing and romanticize guerrilla warfare. The greatest guilt lies with the failed political leadership on both sides of the Atlantic.

Successive Dublin governments have under-estimated the deep interest of many American-Irish in the current tragedy in Northern Ireland. Instead of mobilizing the vast potential of immigrant good will to help resolve the wrongs in Belfast and Derry, Dublin politicians seem to restrict their contact in this country to an endless series of condemnations of American-Irish financial contributions.

If some of America's hard-earned, generously offered dollars have gone to the "wrong hands" in Northern Ireland, the major blame, I would suggest, lies in the unimaginative policymakers of Dublin. They deceive themselves that pandering to a few American politicians is an adequate substitute for establishing working relations with interested academic, religious, athletic, and cultural organiza-tions in this country.

While Israel has carefully courted international involvement in her struggle for freedom and security, the Republic of Ireland, a nation of comparable size and population, has taken an opposite tack, denying her own internal troubles and arrogantly dismissing American concerns.

In a recent poll, less than one percent of the Republic's citizens even listed the conflict in Northern Ireland as a primary problem, and local politicians, faithful to their standards, have not led the masses toward peace. They have sought an easy refuge in the tragic status quo.

The American-Irish community has been no more

fortunate in the political leadership offered by its elected officials. In a land where the Speaker of the House of Representatives and numerous senior senators and leading governors are of Irish extraction, one might have expected some evidence of their influence on government programs aimed at resolving the longest-lasting guerrilla war in western Europe.

Other ethnic groups do not hesitate to use their political clout. Almost thirty percent of all American foreign aid goes to Israel; virtually none goes to Ireland. Preferential Federal legislation permits the transfer of some $750 million a year in tax-exempt charitable contributions to Israel, and other laws permit almost ninety-five percent of Israel's exports to enter the United States duty-free. Military subsidies and other grants cost the American taxpayer billions of dollars annually. There is no similar assistance available to promote Ireland's exports or alleviate her security costs. Approved programs for charitable donations by American-Irish to their homeland are almost non-existent.

American politicians of Irish origin do not seem to share the same ethnic pride or interest in their ancestral home as that which motivates their Jewish congressional colleagues. Annual St. Patrick's Day statements are simply no substitute for concrete acts of assistance:

There are ample precedents to justify a helpful American involvement in the present tragedy in Northern Ireland. In a *Foreign Policy* article several years ago, I offered specific proposals based on established government programs in other parts of the world, where technical assistance, cultural exchange, security supports, and bank and tax credits to promote American investment have all been used to hasten peace in troubled lands. Such programs could—and should—win the same ecumenical support enjoyed by those who have so successfully asked our assistance for Israel and other countries.

The American-Irish community, working in the vacuum created by Dublin and Washington, has failed to channel its emotions into an effective pressure force. Many are unaware of the brutality of everyday life in an area where prejudice, oppression, paranoia, and fear distort every facet of existence.

Too many American-Irish carry on their passionate fights with a courage untouched by personal experience and, far from the carnage, use words and donations that only prolong the agony of those caught in the maelstrom of hatred that flourishes in the ghettos of Northern Ireland today.

There is nothing noble in the killing and maiming of innocent people, or even in the sad waste of the young who take their own lives. Romantic rhetoric cannot excuse indiscriminate violence or justify the sordid obsession in Northern Ireland with useless sacrifice and almost ritual blood-letting.

In contrast with many Americans who glibly comment on the origins and solution of the "troubles" in the north, I have had the unique privilege of teaching medicine in Ireland four times a year for the last fifteen years. My own perspective on Northern Ireland is tempered by a clinician's experience with suffering and pain, and with a deep belief that the very permanence of death solves nothing.

I have shared days with fellow physicians in the emergency rooms of Belfast, known colleagues whose children have been killed by the "brave lads" because their fathers dared to care for the wounds of the enemy, and seen the destruction of a generation etched in the pinched, suspicious faces of women in the Falls Road and Ardoyne ghettos.

From a purely pragmatic point of view, one must reject the failed guerrilla policies of force as well as the Republic's politics of denial. We must emulate the Jewish community and learn to lobby in a forceful manner, so that American politicians will no longer think their obligations are fulfilled by issuing fatuous St. Patrick's Day pronouncements.

It is time that the American-Irish unified their efforts to tear out those blood-red, dark and evil strands of violence that scar the Irish dream, and to initiate cooperative projects that can bring jobs, dignity, and peace to a long-suffering land.

The New York Times, March 11, 1984

American Aid
for Irish Peace

The time has come for the United States to contribute to peace and stability in Northern Ireland as it has done so generously and often elsewhere in the world. The Anglo-Irish Accord, signed last month is, I believe, a historic document. It is, however, short on specifics, and without America's help it may well remain, to paraphrase W.B. Yeats: Words, nothing but words.

The Accord does not purport to settle the conflict: it would give Dublin a symbolic, advisory role in the affairs of Northern Ireland, but it guarantees nothing and offers no detailed program to end the island's civil strife. It promises no new funds or grants and confers no real power on either the Irish Republic or the beleaguered Roman Catholic minority in the north. Nor does it include any plans to reconstruct the bombed-out cities of Derry and Belfast.

It does, however, represent a political device through which peace and security may be achieved. The Accord's purposefully vague declarations of co-operation are all that could be agreed upon now. It did recognize, for the first time, that Dublin has a legitimate right to speak for the Catholic population in the north. This is an important, unprecedented gesture on England's part.

But if these dreams of peace are to become reality, more than fine words and gracious gestures will be necessary. Only steady jobs, decent housing, and equal access to higher education—without which there is neither dignity nor personal freedom—will break the barriers of suspicion and paranoia in Northern Ireland. The success or failure of the Accord will depend ultimately on concrete changes, paid for with material aid—and it is here that America can play an essential role.

It is an unflattering fact of life that America's major role in many international agreements is to cushion the compromises required by sharing our wealth. The Camp David accords, for example, were held together by vast financial aid to both Israel and Egypt. In the same way, in Ireland we ought to be willing to be the silent partner that makes a solution possible.

There are many examples where American aid

has been the glue used to stabilize troubled areas. We have poured hundreds of millions of dollars into Central America so that democracy might survive terrorism and oppression. Why not do the same in Ireland? We have spent hundreds of millions in Cyprus and Turkey to reconstruct towns destroyed by civil war. Why not in Derry? We have allocated more hundreds of millions to build a subway system and upgrade transportation in Cairo. Why not in Belfast? Tax credits and investment guarantees for private American corporations willing to establish facilities in Northern Ireland could be supplemented by the United States. If this has been our national policy elsewhere, why not in Northern Ireland?

The contrast with Israel is most striking. America allocates $3.73 billion a year to Israel, most of it in grants. The usual arguments offered to justify this largesse focus on the strategic significance of Israel and on America's thirty-seven year moral commitment to its survival. But Ireland, too, has made significant contributions to America. The ties between us date back at least three centuries, and Ireland's welfare is of immediate concern to more than forty million American Irish. Nor, surely, is it in our best interest to allow terrorism to flourish in our nearest European neighbor. Yet Ireland receives virtually no government aid from America.

America knows, from her own sad experience, that violence and riots are fed by economic, racial, and religious oppression. Violence is a symptom of social disorder; treat the disease and violence subsides. Give people an effective voice in government and an opportunity to fashion a decent life and they will turn away from those who can rule only by intimidation.

The bitter legacy of history will not suddenly disappear from Northern Ireland. Ancient differences will not easily die and old hatreds take a long time to fade. But tolerance, and the community of shared interests on which it is built, have been achieved in even more difficult situations. There are historic reasons why an American dimension in Northern Ireland, one fully consistent with our current foreign policy elsewhere, is overdue. There are ample precedents to justify a major economic contribution to the present Irish struggle for peace, equality, and justice.

More than a century ago, Charles Steward Parnell, one of the heroes of Ireland's struggle for freedom, appealed to the American Congress: "You can now obtain for Ireland, without the shedding of one drop of blood, without drawing the sword, without one threatening message, the solution of this great question." His words need no amending today. The Anglo-Irish Accord will not work without America's help.

The New York Times, December 26, 1985

SOMALIA

Africa remains the dark continent to most Americans, a vast, unknown land where disasters recur with frightening regularity. Flashing images of starving babies in barren fields, corrupt governments with ever-changing names are the usual perceptions of a television generation that has never had the good fortune to live there. For those who know Africa, it is an incredibly complex, exciting, and enticing place.

Once I walked and worked that area for years on end, studying the diseases of nomads and coming to respect their tradition and culture. More than a quarter century ago I created Somalia's first national health service and have made dozens of research trips to every part of the Horn since then. My findings and experiences have been presented in previous books, *Health on the Horn of Africa* and *Somalia: A Perspective.*

I have included two articles herein that reflect a long-term love affair with Somalia. Scenes of immediate suffering elicit a search for long-term solutions as well as a need for reflection.

Somalia:
Hunger Such
as the World
Had Never Seen

While our national attention was focused some eighteen months ago on the boat people of Vietnam and on those escaping genocide in Cambodia, a sad, steady stream of human refuse had silently fled the war torn Ogaden and was struggling for survival in the harsh, arid Horn of Africa. A half million forgotten people, the victims of famine, oppression, and epidemic illness, were huddled in dry river beds that drought had provided as a home. That was the scene I described in the *Daily News* a year and a half ago to bring to public attention the plight of the largest refugee population in the world.

It was difficult, even for a world full of other problems, to continue ignoring a half million starving refugees, especially when over ninety percent were innocent women and children. Nomadic pride had initially prevented Somalia from seeking international help, but that country, one of the seven poorest on earth, could not long sustain the deluge of refugees. The numbers rapidly grew to over a million, with one out of every five Somalis now living in a refugee camp.

There was genuine humanitarian concern expressed by our nation to this tragedy, but there were also purely pragmatic reasons why the West could ill afford further neglect; Somalia sits astride the Red Sea and has obvious geopolitical significance in the turbulent Indian Ocean and Arabian arena. The light of public attention slowly focused on Somalia, and America became involved.

Our Centers for Disease Control reported a level of malnutrition greater than any previously recorded anywhere, with some thirty-seven percent of the children in one Somali camp suffering from severe protein deficiency. Emergency food shipments from the United States during the early 1980s kept tens of thousands from certain starvation. Voluntary agencies contributed their expertise and assigned enthusiastic young workers to start health, sanitary, and water-supply programs that saved many other thousands from inevitable death by disease. But, as the response to crisis became more organized, the long-term impact of the refugees began to be more fully appreciated.

Somalia had exhausted her meager reserves, and food shortages in the general population became almost as acute as in the camps. The National Health System approached total collapse, and development plans in education, housing, and agriculture were aborted and, in many instances, finally abandoned. Even the landscape may have suffered permanent damage, for refugees have uprooted trees for firewood, eroding the bare plains of precious soil, causing inevitable encroachment by the desert.

I recently attended the United Nations Conference on African Refugees in Geneva where the Reagan administration announced a $285 million commitment for African refugee relief. I then returned to Somalia for meetings with workers in the camps and leaders in the capital. For the past twenty years I have had the privilege of directing annual medical research trips in Somalia, and these steady efforts have secured an unusual, and probably unique, acceptability there. My discussions with Somalis, from the president of the republic to the field worker, are the frank and open exchanges made possible only by hard-won respect and friendship.

Permeating these discussions was a common concern that if the American involvement in disaster relief for refugees is to bring any long-term benefits we must begin to adjust from the current crisis intervention approach to programs that assist in restructuring a fractured society. Transient involvement may, in fact, be even more dangerous than neglect, and unfulfilled promises can leave a bitter legacy, especially in Africa where there is ample experience with self-serving opportunists. Ill-conceived programs may do far more harm than the brief benefits they offer.

This transition from crisis aid to development

emphasis may be difficult for some, for world attention is fickle; the problems of the moment have dramatic appeal but, no matter how severe, can be soon forgotten. Yet the essence of international relief work demands flexibility and humility.

It is impossible, for example, to regulate the customs of a people. Refugee food supplies donated by the United States do not include camel milk or dates or goat meat, the staples of a nomad diet. An effective barter system has emerged in Somalia with refugees trading some of their subsistence for more traditional foods or for essentials such as soap and clothes. This adaptation of donations permits the refugee a minimum of human dignity, yet it brings criticism from those who demand a rigid accounting for every parcel of aid provided.

The hospital system of Somalia is presently in chaos, with more medicines, equipment, and expatriate staff in some of the camps than in the cities. The camps depend on the hospitals for critical back-up care; the success of one is inextricably entwined with the other, for disease has no boundaries. Yet some international medical programs are imposing artificial barriers that limit their contribution only to the refugees. Immunization campaigns, for example, can prevent illness but not if they touch only a part of the exposed population.

The Somalis are a resilient people; they have had to be merely to survive as nomads in the desert. In recent years their nation has been ravaged by war, drought, and the largest refugee population in the world. America is now responding generously to the Somali appeal for help, and if our aid is wisely planned the benefits will be felt by future generations of Somalis as well as by the current victims of famine.

The Horn of Africa may be poor today, but it has vast potential with millions of acres of untouched land, with untapped mineral resources and the largest coastline in Africa. The friends we win today in the heat of their battle for life will not forget. They might be the critical factor in stablilizing a troubled world for our own children tomorrow.

The New York Daily News, April 23, 1982

Palm Sunday
in Somalia

When the Nazarene entered Jerusalem astride a
donkey, and the crowds placed palms before his
feet, a ceremony of welcome was begun that has been
renewed annually for almost two thousand years. The
Gospels tell us of the many varied faces that came
together in those narrow tropical streets to see the
Messiah—dark Africans, those from Galilee and
Cyrene, slaves and aristocrats from all sectors of the
Roman Empire.

It may be difficult to recapture the vibrancy of that
scene when, well-nourished and well-dressed, we
hear the Passion recounted through a microphone,
and gather our palms at the rear of a church before
joining neighbors for a walk in the comfort and
security of America. Somehow we seem to have lost
the poetry that comes with the cacophony of sounds
that are part of the tropics. One might think that the
earthy smells and the hot, moist climate would crush
the joy and spirit of Palm Sunday, but two weeks ago
in Somalia I found a vitality, sincerity, and beauty that
we in America would do well to emulate.

I attended Palm Sunday services in the old Italian Cathedral in the capital city of Mogadiscio. Its twin stone towers are the tallest points in that ancient Islamic port on the Indian ocean; the towers have become landmarks for relief workers who are coming in ever growing numbers to help the largest refugee population in the world today. Volunteers from all over the world have begun to open their hearts and give assistance to an almost forgotten people in an utterly neglected part of Africa.

I have had the lonely privilege of making annual medical research trips in Somalia for the past twenty years. When I was last in the refugee camps a year and a half ago there were a half million refugees gathered in the makeshift camps. Over ninety percent were women and children, and the smell of death was pervasive. There was virtually no foreign assistance, with only three medical volunteers in the entire country.

Today the onslaught continues. Over three thousand new refugees arrive daily and the total camp population now exceeds 1,300,000. Famine, drought, and epidemic disease take their toll, but the number of refugees still steadily increases. The world is now beginning to respond with hundreds of volunteers sharing in the crisis, and charitable agencies from Europe and America are providing food and medicine in many camps. Catholic Relief Service has health teams in the Lugh area, one of the most severely affected zones.

This year on Palm Sunday, Somali Catholics were joined in their procession around the Cathedral by followers of Christ from many lands, men and women who had come to serve the refugees. There were Indian and Asian workers; young Swedish and American volunteers mixed with the Italian and English residents who had stayed to bridge the gap between colonial and modern independent Africa.

Despite stultifying heat the Bishop was in full regalia, for this was a celebration initiating Holy Week. The white cassocks of friars, nuns, and altar boys blended well with the casual, cool garb of the sweating congregation. But neither insects nor weather could suppress the spirit, and there was an almost palpable sense of common involvement that reminded me of the spirit that must have pervaded the palm-lined streets of Jerusalem so long ago.

Catholic New York, April 23, 1984

AIDS AND SUFFERING

This final section considers challenges that are defined by neither geography nor regional political interests; the global fear of AIDS and the personal experience of death know no restrictions.

The ultimate victim in every disaster is a person. The intensity of this fundamental—and harsh—truth is often diffused, for it is emotionally easier to emphasize the vague sufferings of society or the impersonal damage to a nation. Yet it is always a specific human being who feels pain and dies. Nowhere has this been seen more clearly in recent years than in *The AIDS Epidemic,* a title I gave to the first scientific volume devoted to this scourge.

Here the isolation and rejection of the patient were matched by the frustration of the physician, for neither could depend on those magical tools of modern medicine we had all come to take for granted. In the loneliness of our new—and humbling—position we have begun to re-learn the meanings of dignity and hope and even, as in my final article, the spiritual nobility that can be found in suffering and death.

Reflections
on the AIDS
Epidemic*

For the past eight years I have had the opportunity to discuss the clinical and therapeutic aspects of AIDS with physicians in many hospitals in the United States and abroad. I should like to focus here upon some of the social and philosophic issues that have been raised, at least for me, by the AIDS experience.

I would like to begin with a story, a story whose relevance to the topic at hand may not be immediately evident. It is the story about the government scientists who were conducting an experiment on frogs and their ability to leap great distances.

First they trained the frog to leap on their com-

Demographics updated to January 1988.

77

mand, "jump," and took measurements of the distance covered. Next, they cut off one of the frog's legs, gave it the command, "jump," and again measured the result. Then, a second leg was cut off and a third, followed each time by the command, "jump," and a measurement of the distance covered. Finally, they amputated the frog's fourth leg. But when they gave it the command, "jump," nothing happened. It just sat there staring ahead.

The scientists went back to their office and wrote their report. Its conclusion was that "cutting off all four legs of a frog makes it go deaf."

Reduced to its simplest terms, that is, I suppose, a story about cause and effect, or more precisely, about the kind of absurdity—or at least inappropriate reaction—that can result, in medicine as well as in laboratory experiments, when people substitute subjective opinion for the evidence at hand.

That lesson, sadly, was part of what we learned as the AIDS epidemic evolved. Reaction and hypotheses and even conclusions usually reflected more on the mores and fears of the instant authorities who emerged almost daily than on the few facts that were available.

At one end of the spectrum, there were those who were all too ready to see the disease as a punishment from on high. To this group, the cause was clear: the homosexual lifestyle of the victims. The effect, a pestilence brought on by the wrath of God, was justified even if it was, in their view, a bit late coming on.

At the other extreme were gay activists, some of whom saw the disease as an opportunity to advocate what were essentially social and political, not medical, gains for the homosexual community. A few even suggested that the cause of this epidemic was man-made, that someone or some group was waging chemical or biological warfare against gays.

Government's reaction to the epidemic was also puzzling, especially at first. Epidemics of the recent past had triggered an immediate, huge response on the part of the federal government. The homosexuals claimed, with some justification, that the response to the AIDS epidemic was sluggish in the extreme and was influenced adversely by the sexual preferences of the victims.

When Government did respond, it did so—in part at least—inappropriately. The city government in New York set up Offices of Gay and Lesbian Health, thereby exhibiting, it seems to me, a serious confusion of medical and social problems and establishing a precedent that, logically pursued, would lead to the proliferation of health offices, each devoted to the concerns of a narrowly defined population. This expedient political decision, presumably intended to curry favor among activists for homosexual rights, forced AIDS victims who had, for example, acquired their fatal disease from transfusion, to seek official help from an office that represented an ethos they found offensive.

Early in the epidemic, four groups were identified

79

as being particularly susceptible to AIDS: homosexual men, intravenous drug users, hemophiliacs, and Haitians. The inclusion of Haitians among the at-risk groups set off other reactions in which there seemed to be little relation between cause and effect. Some Haitians claimed that their inclusion was racially motivated. Although there is no evidence to support that charge, the Haitian community-at-large did suffer from their identification as an at-risk group. Haitian children were taunted at school, and Haitian workers, especially those employed as domestic help, found their jobs threatened because of the fear, completely unsubstantiated, that they might carry and transmit AIDS.

This epidemic then, was wrapped from the beginning in layers of confusion and twisted logic. Like the scientists in the frog story, people seemed to draw from the facts whatever conclusions suited their convenience or purposes.

Having begun with those thoughts, let us look now at some of the terrible facts of the AIDS epidemic. Several years ago, healthy young men began to die in large numbers from an unknown disease. As so often happens in the history of medicine, the early cases were considered isolated extremes in the normal spectrum of any illness and there was, in retrospect, an inadequate appreciation by the health professions of a growing disaster. Slowly, but inexorably, the numbers who were afflicted grew until this insidious disease exploded into a frightening epidemic.

Persons who had been previously well, developed rare tumors and unusual systemic infections. Studies indicated that these patients had suddenly and inexplicably lost their normal immunity to disease. They had an illness for which modern medicine had no name and, in our ignorance, we called it Acquired Immune Deficiency Syndrome—or AIDS.

Many years ago an Irish poet captured in rhyme the chaos that follows the destruction in a human being of something so basic as our protective immunologic system. The poet's words seem applicable as well to the social stresses that flowed from our fear of the unknown. In *The Second Coming*, Yeats wrote:

Turning and turning in the widening gyre
The falcon cannot hear the falconer.
Things fall apart; the center cannot hold;
Mere anarchy is loosed upon the world,
The blood-dimmed tide is loosed,
   and everywhere
The ceremony of innocence is drowned;
The best lack all conviction, while the worst
Are full of passionate intensity.

More and more cases of AIDS have been recognized since it was first seen in 1979-80. At first, all the victims were homosexual men in New York City and California, but soon heterosexual Haitians and drug addicts were diagnosed as having the disease. Then blood recipients, particularly hemophiliacs, fell before this new, puzzling, and deadly epidemic. The numbers have steadily doubled every six months. By January 1988 the United States Centers for Disease Control had verified over fifty thousand American cases; AIDS has also been documented overseas in virtually every country from Scandinavia to Japan. In eastern and central Africa, AIDS has been a national calamity, affecting, in some areas, over ten percent of the population.

As the epidemic spread there were many questions and few answers. Concern led to fear and mushroomed into panic. There were demands for drastic action but no one was quite certain what to do.

United States federal officials seemed to approach the epidemic with embarrassment, declaring that the problem was a local issue; local authorities claimed they could do little without national support. Words and endless meetings became a substitute for rational action. Politicians handled the epidemic with unaccustomed wariness. Almost without exception public leaders evaded the epidemic, avoiding even the usual expressions of compassion and concern. It was as if the sexual orientation of the victims made any involvement risky, and the politicians directed their courage and energies elsewhere.

In the spring of 1983 I had the privilege of chairing a major symposium on AIDS in New York. Colleagues —including the directors of the United States Centers for Disease Control and of our National Institutes of Health, the presidents of the Infectious Disease Society of America and of the American Blood Bank Association, concerned Health Commissioners and fellow clinicians—gathered to detail the then known facts about AIDS. Despite an unusually close relationship with a fair number of our senior senators and congressmen, I could not entice a single one of them even to identify with our impeccable scientific session.

A single act, the compassionate deed of a saintly man, crumbled that shameful wall of official reticence. I approached the late Terence Cardinal Cooke, Archbishop of New York, and told him how the politicians were avoiding involvement, possibly because of a fear that Church figures might be critical of any support for the homosexual community. His Eminence immediately responded by offering to open the symposium himself, and from that moment on the politicians issued endless pronouncements and the media dramatized the epidemic almost to a point that we longed for the quiet and lonely days of a year ago.

Still the young men continued to die. In New York City alone, we have had over fifteen thousand cases, with an eighty percent mortality in those patients diagnosed two years ago. My own personal experience is no different; because of my interest in parasitic diseases I have seen an inordinate number of AIDS patients. They are—as a group—the most difficult patients I have ever managed, for as one succeeds in controlling a critical infection another complication emerges. In my own personal series of over five hundred cases, few have survived three years.

But even as the disaster escalated, the organized medical community was strangely absent. When a fatal infection had struck down veterans attending an American Legion convention, health professionals across the country joined in the search for a solution. When women using tampons became ill with toxic shock syndrome, medical societies and research centers immediately focused their enormous talents on that problem. But when the victims were drug addicts and poor Haitian refugees and homosexual men, their plight did not, somehow, seem so significant to those expected to speak for the health professions. No major research programs were announced in the first two years of the AIDS epidemic and, until it became clear that the disease could spread to the general population through blood transfusions, organized medicine seemed part of the curious conspiracy of silence.

Nevertheless, when historians reflect on this epidemic years hence, I suspect they will not stress the sordid stories of failure and neglect, but rather will recount the remarkable tales of heroism that illuminate this dark, lonely period of struggle to unravel the unknown.

While government and organized medicine appeared to look for excuses for inaction, a new collective strength was building among those most at risk of contracting AIDS. Their greatest strength lay in a determination not to be destroyed, in a will that demanded public attention be paid to this epidemic, and in an unprecedented willingness to help those who needed the medical, psychological, and social assistance that society had not offered. Out of such determination was formed the Gay Men's Health Crisis and other groups that have done superb work educating, advising, and sustaining frightened, vulnerable people with nowhere else to turn.

No one has captured better than Albert Camus the unique exile an epidemic imposes. In *The Plague* he wrote:

> There was always something missing in their lives. Hostile to the past, impatient of the present, and cheated of the future, we were much like those whom men's justice, or hatred, forces to live behind prison bars.... The plague had swallowed up everything and everyone. No longer were there individual destinies, only a collective destiny, made of plague and the emotions shared by all. Strongest of these emotions was the sense of exile and of deprivation, with all the cross-currents of revolt and fear set up by these.

All too often the victims of AIDS have been made to feel like Camus's victims, exiled and deprived of the full measure of what modern medicine can offer. But there have also been many instances of individual courage, of simple adherence by physicians and nurses and technicians to a code as old as medicine itself. These will never be recorded or acknowledged individually. Clinical medicine is not built on heroic deeds or memorable feats but on steady, loyal service to patients. When those patients are dying in large numbers and when the mode of transmission of their disease is unknown, then the daily routine of involved health workers assumes a quiet dignity and decency that deserves special respect.

The clinician has an unusual role in an epidemic, for he or she shares the victims' sufferings, their despair, and their dwindling hopes. In this epidemic, we, as physicians, have had daily to face patients in the prime of life who are suffering from a disease we do not understand and cannot cure. We have often had to sustain them solely with the ancient commitment of our profession to remain at our posts seeking answers and offering help until this modern plague has been conquered. There is usually nothing dramatic in service, except in retrospect.

Camus's fictional physician, Dr. Rieux, had noted, in the midst of their epidemic:

> an inability to record at this point something of a really spectacular order—some heroic feat or memorable deed like those that thrill us in the chronicles of the past. The truth is that nothing is less sensational than pestilence, and by reason of their very duration great misfortunes are monotonous. In the memories of those who lived through them, the grim days of plague do not stand out like

vivid flames, ravenous and inextinguishable, beaconing a troubled sky, but rather like a slow, deliberate progress of some monstrous thing crushing out all upon its path.

Even if we as physicians are incapable, at least for a time, of altering the inexorable progress of an epidemic, we have nonetheless a very priviliged position from which to view the vagaries of man. Is that privilege appreciated and utilized? Too often the answer must be "No." For too long, medical professionals have spoken only to one another—documenting the toll of disease, studying its causes and victims, calling upon everyone to listen to their advice.

They have failed, however, to move beyond the traditional limitations of the profession, failed to realize that merely convincing—or is it conversing with?—one another has neither altered economic policies nor significantly influenced political will, and it is in these areas that the critical decisions that determine the extent or even existence, of health programs are made most frequently. Too rarely have competent, respected health experts been willing to venture into the turbulent councils where government priorities are established and financial allocations are set. Those best qualified have made too small a contribution to these councils in regard to the human resource, the human potential, and the impact of programs on people.

If there has been a sense of outrage at the human

condition, whether in the AIDS epidemic or in any other disaster, those who should be most able to express this have either been unable or unwilling to articulate the harsh realities of sickness in comprehensible terms that can alter the opinions and actions of decision-makers. For too long we who deal with and know most intimately the one unique resource—the human being—have allowed our project to remain dreams, and our priorities to be words. If professionals in science and health continue merely to rail against the system and arrogantly absent themselves from the political process they should not have—and do not deserve—the power to fashion our society.

Reflecting on the social and philosophic aspects of the AIDS experience provides, I suggest, an unusual opportunity for perspective as well as a chance to rekindle the spirit of a community. This is not the worst disaster I have seen, for I have had the rare fortune of directing health services in Somali refugee camps where over a million women and children were starving; and I was once in charge of medical relief services after the Nicaraguan earthquakes when nearly twenty thousand people died in a night. I have run clinics while bombs fell on our building in West Beirut. Some perspective is needed as we deal with the AIDS epidemic.

Each generation deludes itself by thinking that the demands imposed on it are more rigorous than those that predecessors had to bear, that the problems are more insoluble now than then, that it is suffering a complexity in human life never before encountered, that far more is expected of its members than was of those before them. And speakers often encourage this delusion by sending their listeners off with the charge to resolve the problems that their fathers created.

All of this somehow does not ring true to experience. It denies the continuity of human life. It is too naive a view of the world. People have always needed to struggle. Right never triumphed spontaneously over wrong. Integrity has always been maintained only through acts of courage. Compassion has never been worth a damn unless it manifested itself in concrete acts of love.

Our own day is no different. Only the morally blind can miss the symbols of sacrifice in our world. They are everywhere: on a wall in Belfast, where a child has scratched the desperate question, "Is there a life before death?"; in the hollow eye sockets and the mocking, bloated bellies of those dying from malnutrition in Bangladesh, in Africa, and in Latin America; and, surely, in the hopeless faces of AIDS patients who appear increasingly like Auschwitz prisoners as they inexorably approach death.

We must not allow ourselves to become so well insulated by distance and by our own good fortune that we never feel the chill reality of others' sufferings. We must not allow the facts of hunger and poverty, of disease and political despotism to remain merely statistics and forget that it is people, not numbers, that get sick, and are starving and oppressed. We must not merely talk about problems and deceive ourselves that words—or even concern—are substitutes for corrective actions and deeds of compassion.

It may seem that I have wandered far from the AIDS patient, but it is essential for us to realize that his medical care has been, and is, influenced by forces that have nothing to do with immunology or chemotherapy; he is the beneficiary, or the victim, of all our views of illness and life, of the priorities we set in allocating public funds and of the perspective that both past experiences and future dreams impose on our society.

In addition to the medical challenge of AIDS in the United States there has been a growing crisis in hospitals and social service departments. Because of the need for isolation precautions, every facet of the care of an AIDS patient, from nursing and nutrition to laboratory work and housekeeping, becomes extremely costly. The duration of an AIDS patient's hospital stay is usually measured in months: many of my patients have passed over seventy five percent of the last year of their young lives wasting away in the solitary confinement of an isolation cell. Hospital bills in excess of four hundred thousand dollars, now occur with regularity. Health insurance coverage for the young and poor, who constitute the majority of AIDS victims, is usually inadequate, often non-existent in the United States. Society had not planned for this epidemic.

Nevertheless, the history of medicine reassures

us that, somehow, with time and effort, the terrible mystery of AIDS will be unraveled and a cure will be found. When that day comes, we may look back and reflect with the same satisfaction that Camus's character, Dr. Rieux, experienced as the epidemic finally vanished from Oran:

> And it was in the midst of shouts rolling against the terrace wall in massive waves that waxed in volume and duration, while cataracts of colored fire fell thicker through the darkness, that Dr. Rieux resolved to compile this chronicle, so that he should not be one of those who hold their peace but should bear witness in favor of those plague-stricken people; so that some memorial of the injustice and outrage done them might endure; and to state quite simply what we learn in time of pestilence; that there are more things to admire in men than to despise.

The AIDS epidemic forcefully reminds us of both the humility and nobility inherent in our humanity.

Journal of The Irish Colleges of Physicians and Surgeons, October, 1984

A Physician
Views Suffering
and Pain

A physician's view of suffering is tempered by constant exposure to pain. While philosophers and theologians may ponder the societal value of suffering, the medical doctor must deal daily with the evils of uncontrolled pain, and help to resolve in the individual patient the apparent tension between theological theory and clinical reality.

The control of pain is the fundamental mandate of medicine. The incredibly rich history of medicine—possibly the noblest record of human activity—is the tale of an endless search for the means to free the patient from the destructive impact of pain.

One of the foundations of modern medicine was the discovery of anaesthesia in the 19th century. Only then could prolonged surgery be performed, and complicated childbirth, for example, be managed with care. Until that time pain was always the limiting factor; panic a predictable response; shock or death the inevitable result.

Medicine has evolved as both a science and an art. The ability to measure observations, to objectively record impressions, to devise specific techniques that allow comparisons over time—these are the essential methods of the science of medicine. One can, for example, determine the extent of damage to a heart muscle through the tracing of an electrocardiogram, and measure the amount of morphine required to eradicate the sensation of pain. But in dealing with pain, the science of medicine does not have the tools to measure a victim's concerns, or fears, or suffering.

Each patient brings to his or her illness a certain cultural and personal influence. It is through an understanding of the mystery of the patient's uniqueness that the good physician practices the art of medicine. This elusive quality of medicine, a most subtle experience, permits the physician to share in the patient's suffering while simultaneously alleviating pain.

Last year, the Archbishop of New York, Terence Cardinal Cooke, referred to his last few months on earth as a "grace-filled time of my life." It was a time when the world watched a saintly man approach death while celebrating life in a series of memorable messages. It was also a time of agonizing pain distilled into edifying suffering. For the physician it was a time when the science and the art of medicine coalesced.

Pain was an evil whose wince and grimace and cry could not be made romantic by any rhetoric; it had to be conquered so that the Cardinal could continue the life he loved and prepare, through prayer and suffering, for the eternal reward he sought. Drugs had to be constantly titrated so that pain could be tolerated without sacrificing the mental clarity so necessary for his final contributions. The patient who experiences that creative tension between suffering and pain must be sustained by both the art and the science of medicine. Thus, the perspective of the physician is indispensable to even the spiritual assessment of this complex and universal experience.

Catholic Near East, October 10, 1984

A View of the Author:
The Medicine Man

by Leonard Bernstein

Doctors (we do not here include them all, of course, and make a mental reservation of certain admirable exceptions) are in general more displeased, more irritated by the invalidation of their verdicts than pleased by their execution.

Marcel Proust

Now behold the admirable exception supreme, Dr. Kevin M. Cahill. Nothing pleases him more than a surprise recovery, or displeases him more, to a point of personal anguish, then to have "tried everything" and then have to stand helplessly by, watching the inevitable "execution of the verdict."

It is hard not to love Kevin; it is equally hard to know which Kevin you are loving. He is that complicated creature once called a "Medicine Man," a term that presents us with a host of dualities: pillar of society/leprechaun; medieval alchemist/medical master; shaman/clinician; witchdoctor/psychologist; juggler/saint. I have observed him in all these phases, I think; I have appeared at his office in despair, begging for some magic pill, only to leave like Fred Astaire, lighter than air, with not even a placebo to con me on my way. How does this happen? What went on in there during that hour or more, aside from a cardiogram, some palpation, and what I think of as the *Stethoscopic Follies*, the shortest show in New York. Oh yes, the prerequisite blood sample; but all that surely didn't take an hour plus. Of course not; we *talked*.

Now, we are both Talkers (and Listeners), but our conversations sometimes get a bit out of control; we always seem to have fascinating tales to tell, and between my rabbinical streak and his Blarney Connection we sometimes need a referee. But what needs to get done gets done, because his intuitive insights are remarkable. Proof: Here I sit writing about him, smoking cigarettes at 3:00 a.m. and feeling not too bad, as I peer into the clouded crystal ball of my seventies. And Kevin sometimes even comes to my concerts, and acts as if he really enjoys them, although my guess is that he knows as much about Mahler as I do about salmonella.

It occurs to me suddenly that my tone in this

afterword is rather more chatty, more lightweight than a contribution should be to a profoundly serious, even grievous, book. These essays are, after all, concerned with life, death, and the never-ending shock of war. But I think that the multifaceted nature of the man Cahill is of such interest that making this "frontal attack" can only enhance what has been read by bringing his image(s) to the fore, his presence to the reader. And so I will linger a bit longer on the man Cahill, the lovable and, yes, vulnerable, Kevin Cahill.

One way to observe him (which may help to flesh out the Medicine Man image) is to place yet another identification tag on his breastpocket: The Family Man. I don't know how he does it, but he does find time, lots of it, to be close to all his rather unusual family—his beautiful wife and five (!) sons, for starters. There are cousins, brothers too, but he is never too busy to advise, comfort, guide, and ease the way for any and all. His idea of Heaven is an *omnium gatherum* of these descendants of the Irish Bronx of yore, carefully guided by St. Ignatius Loyola. Sheer Jesuitical bliss, including the progressively problematic young manhood of five male siblings. Birthdays, Christmas, graduations are all taken very seriously; but the *omnissium gatherissimum* of all has to be seen to be believed—the occasion of the annual dinner of the American Irish Historical Society, of which Kevin is President-General. There, at that medallion-awarding dinner at the Waldorf, standing proudly on his five-and-one-half feet, surrounded by family, in-laws, friends, and cronies, grateful patients, the Irish and the non-Irish (I've attended twice and I'm not even Welsh)—there and then, at that event, we may sense something different, something even larger than the Medicine Man: The Miracle Man. What you sense there is that his close family has increased exponentially; you have the feeling that *everyone* there is in some way a brother, sister, parent, or child of Kevin Cahill. How he manages them all I can't imagine. It's the Loaves and Fishes, for Pete's sake.

Then let your imagination travel out from the Waldorf Grand Ballroom in every direction and see this family multiply and diversify even more, be it in Somalia, Nicaragua, the Vatican, a variety of hospitals and medical schools from Lenox Hill to Dublin, even to my aging secretary's sickbed in her own apartment —everywhere he goes his amazingly large family keeps expanding. They love him, they are his family, because he loves them. I don't think it hyperbolic to say that he dispenses loving care on every individual who needs him *medically*, from the Pope to my secretary; and they respond in kind. (I wish we could find a suitable substitute for that abused, misused four-letter word, *love*, but it won't give in.) Moreover, he is loved by many who do *not* need his medical care, but love him anyway. You see, that four-letter word just won't go away.

When I agreed to write this section I envisaged a solemn commentary on this latest collection of Dr. Cahill's essays, all of which I had read in one form or another. But now, upon rereading them in this order, I find that they have combined into a unity, a kind of prayer book or breviary—a Mass applicable to any faith, or even non-faith. It strikes me as a Sequence leading ultimately to communion and benediction. I now read the AIDS piece as an Offertory, the Nicaragua pieces as a Credo, before each of which I find myself murmuring a premature *Amen*.